The
GOLDEN AGE
of
OCEAN
LINERS

LEE SERVER

SMITHMARK

This edition published in 1996 by SMITHMARK Publishers,
a division of U.S. Media Holdings, Inc.
16 East 32nd Street
New York, NY 10016

SMITHMARK books are available for bulk purchase
for sales promotion and premium use.

For details write or call the manager of special sales,
SMITHMARK Publishers
16 East 32nd Street
New York, NY 10016
(212) 532-6600

This book was designed and produced by
Todtri Productions Limited
P.O. Box 572
New York, NY 10116-0572
FAX: (212) 279-1241

Printed and bound in Singapore

Library of Congress Catalog Card Number 96-68011
ISBN 0-7651-9776-6

Author: Lee Server

Publisher: Robert M. Tod
Editorial Director: Elizabeth Loonan
Designer and Art Director: Ron Pickless
Production Coordinator: Heather Weigel
Senior Editor: Edward Douglas
Project Editor: Cynthia Sternau
Associate Editor: Shawna Kimber
Picture Researchers: Julie Dewitt, Natalie Goldstein,
    Kate Lewin, Cathy Stastny
Research Assistant: Laura Wyss
Typeset and DTP: Blanc Verso/UK

PICTURE CREDITS

AKG Photo, London pp. 14, 17, 19 (bottom), 24–25, 28, 29 (top), 30, 60

Bulloz Photographic pp. 7, 35 (top)

Jean-Loup Charmet pp. 15 (top), 44 (bottom), 47 (top), 52, 54, 58–59, 69

Corbis-Bettmann pp. 37, 41, 53 (top & bottom), 57, 66

Cunard Line pp. 8–9, 79 (bottom)

Edimedia pp. 4, 47 (bottom)

Editions Tallandier Phototheque pp. 21 (bottom), 29 (bottom), 32 (bottom), 33, 35 (bottom), 46 (top)

e.t. archive p. 50

Mary Evans Picture Library pp. 6, 12, 16 (top & bottom), 27, 48, 55, 56, 67

Hulton Deutsch p. 69

The Kobal Collection pp. 70, 71 (top & bottom), 72 (bottom), 76 (bottom), 77

The Metropolitan Museum of Art p. 34

Museum of the City of New York pp. 13, 18, 19 (top), 22 (top left & right), 22 (bottom), 23, 26 (top), 38, 39 (top & bottom), 40, 43 (top & bottom), 44 (top), 49 (top & bottom)

Nawrocki Stock Photo pp. 78–79

New York Public Library pp. 15 (bottom), 21 (top), 42, 46 (bottom), 61 (left), 62

Photofest pp. 72 (top), 73, 74 (top), 75, 76 (top)

Photo Artephot/R. Perrin pp. 36

The Ritz, London p. 20

Springer/Corbis-Bettmann pp. 10, 74 (bottom)

Topham Picture Source pp. 5, 31, 45, 61 (right)

UPI/Corbis-Bettmann pp. 25 (top & bottom), 26 (bottom), 32 (top), 49 (center), 51, 63 (top & bottom), 64, 65

CONTENTS

ℐNTRODUCTION

Opposite: While the liners of the North Atlantic lanes are the most famous of the era, luxurious passenger ships served numerous other world routes. The Matson Navigation Company's *Malolo*, shown here in a painting, carried passengers between California and Hawaii.

Along New York's Hudson River piers today there are few indications of a once glorious past. Only ghosts and a few crumbling structures remain to evoke that time—the heyday of the great ocean liners between the two world wars—when the western edge of Manhattan Island met the massive dark hulls and gleaming superstructures of these extraordinary ships. It was an era when ports around the world hummed with the activity, excitement, and glamour of a golden age in transoceanic travel.

For more than half a century—until the growth of commercial jet service in the late 1950s—the great passenger liners were the predominant means of crossing the world's oceans. In the age-old history of shipping, they were vessels of unprecedented size and speed, comfort, and safety. The liners made possible the efficient and economical movement of vast numbers of people from one continent to another. But, in their heyday, these colossal craft were much more than merely a successful new means of transportation.

The liners held a place of pride in the human spirit. From the time of the launching of the first superliner, the *Kaiser Wilhelm der Grosse*, in 1897, the ships were seen—rivaled only by the big city skyscrapers—as the modern

Below: Not as well known as the *France*, *Paris*, or *Île de France*, the *Pasteur* nevertheless provided the same high standard of French style and service.

equivalent to the man-made wonders of the ancient world. With some vessels measuring over one thousand feet in length, reaching speeds of over 30 knots, and traversing the fierce North Atlantic in under a week, the liners were the remarkable emblems of a remarkable era, symbols of the machine age, and of the seemingly limitless progress of science and technology.

Many of the ships became legendary—the *Leviathan*, *Queen Mary*, *Mauretania*, and the *Normandie*. These were names known even to those who had never set eyes on an ocean let alone an ocean liner. Some others—most notably the doomed *Titanic*—became watchwords for tragedy and symbols of another sort, vivid proof that nature still reigned supreme over modern man's most remarkable achievements.

Like the railroads and the steamboats had in the 1800s, the ocean liners played an important role in the history of the early twentieth century. They opened new worlds for millions of travelers from sightseers to settlers, and permitted enormous changes in

ABONNEMENTS

Trois mois	Six mois	Un an
FRANCE & COLONIES
4 fr. | 7 fr. 50 | 14 fr.
UNION POSTALE
6 fr. | 12 fr. | 22 fr.

Le Petit Journal
—— illustré ——

PARAISSANT LE DIMANCHE
33ᵉ Année - Nᵒ 1654
On s'abonne dans tous
les bureaux de poste
Les Manuscrits ne sont pas rendus

Une voyageuse hardie

Bien que transportée en avion, une jeune Américaine arrive à Cherbourg trop tard pour prendre
le paquebot. Mais aussitôt elle frète une rapide vedette, rejoint en mer le transatlantique
et monte à bord, à la force des poignets, le long d'une corde qui lui est lancée.

global commerce and communications.

The liners were a critical factor in the population growth of the "New World" nations in the first decades of the century. Countless Europeans who had immigrated to America (and in lesser numbers to Australia, Canada, and South America) experienced passage on one of the giant ocean-going ships. Until the passing of more restrictive laws on immigration in 1921, the liners carried over one million emigrants per year to the port of New York City alone. These poor travelers, in search of new lives, came by third or steerage class, the cheapest ticket. This provided decidedly no-frills service and accommodations in the ship's lowest decks, with dormitories crammed with hard bunks for sleeping, and Spartan communal areas for everything else. While the emigrants' tickets were relatively low in cost, their sheer numbers made them extremely valuable to the shipping companies. It was in large part to profit from the endless stream of third class passengers that the fleets of ocean liners were built in the 1900s. Without them, the massive immigration to the United States that took place in this period would never have been possible.

Away from the much-trafficked North Atlantic routes, the giant liners traveling between Europe, Asia, and Africa expedited another form of immigration. The European empires with their distant colonies, particularly Great Britain and its vast bureaucratic rule of the Indian subcontinent, sent off colonists, officers, farmers, merchants and civil servants by the

Opposite: The activities of the 1920s international smart set were endlessly reported. Here, a wealthy American woman is determined not to miss her ship as it sails from Cherbourg for home.

Below: The dazzling *Horse Taming* occupied the starboard side of the *Normandie*'s smoking room. The artist, Dunand, was one of the world's preeminent coppersmiths before he began working in lacquer.

Left: The *Queen Elizabeth II*, commissioned in 1969, is thought of as the last of the floating palaces. Here we see the ship's elegant Caronia dining room.

Above: A luncheon at the captain's table is faithfully reenacted for the 1958 film *A Night to Remember*, based on Walter Lord's bestseller about the *Titanic* tragedy.

thousands. The liners carried these men and women—and sometimes all of their furniture as well—on the long journey to Bombay, Singapore, or Hong Kong, and a year later—or three or even ten years later—took most of them on board again for the journey back home. The shipboard commute to and from India was such a familiar experience for the British during this period that a term known to veteran colonial voyagers entered the common language: The word "posh," now meaning something elegant and superior, derived from the acronym "Port Out Starboard Home," signifying the more desirable, and cooler, cabins for each stage of the journey.

When the era of mass immigration to the United States came to a close in the early 1920s, the shipping companies experienced a large drop in revenue. In short order they began retooling their fleets and promoted them to the public with another class of passenger foremost in mind. While the great liners had always been distinguished by the splendor of their first class service, they now sought to outdo themselves with an unprecedented form of luxury.

The new and newly refurbished ocean liners of the Roaring Twenties emphasized high style and opulence above all. They featured grand ballrooms, huge, high-ceilinged dining rooms (with spectacular dining to match), nightclubs, and suites that compared with the most elaborate of grand hotel penthouses. There was every sort of special interest salon, smoking rooms, stately libraries, and theaters for screening the latest Hollywood productions. The design and decor of the new ships such as the *Île de France*, *Europa*, and *Lafayette* made them aesthetic showpieces for the dazzling and futuristic styles known as Art Deco and Streamline. Their influence was such that motifs drawn from the great Art-Deco liners appeared in resort hotels, bus stations, movie theaters, automobiles, appliances, and elsewhere.

Life aboard ship in this era was literally in the lap of luxury, from the attentions of the strictly-trained and crisply-outfitted staff, and the nightly serenading by a live orchestra, to the consuming of elaborate gourmet meals, fine wines, and liquors. This hedonistic approach to ship travel became all-encompassing with the development of the "pleasure cruise"—long, lingering journeys on vessels designed for the sunny skies of the tropics, the Caribbean, the Mediterranean, the South Pacific. Numerous lines advertised luxurious round-the-world cruises, appealing primarily to the "idle rich" who could afford the cost and time of a voyage lasting upwards of five months.

The luxury of the most famous liners invariably attracted (and was invariably publicized by the lines themselves) the presence of a rarefied group of passengers that included royalty, movie stars, industrial magnates, and other celebrities of the day. The notion of crossing paths and wining and dining with the rich and famous made a first class ocean voyage still more appealing for those "ordinary" travelers who could afford it. In fact, during this glossiest period of luxury liner travel, even a second class or the newly contrived tourist class passage (replacing steerage) was imbued with an undeniable glamour.

It was indeed difficult for anyone to escape the romance of the luxury liners in the 1920s and 1930s. Upscale magazines were filled with slick, stylish advertisements trumpeting the comforts and colorful life on board the *Franconia*, the *Homeric*—all "the splendid ships of the United States Line!"—and many more. Radio and newsreels diligently covered each celebrity-studded champagne christening of a new vessel and reported the latest Blue Riband winner in the race for the fastest Atlantic crossing. Books and especially the movies promoted the hedonistic life aboard ship. Filmgoers could watch Fred Astaire and Ginger Rogers and other cinematic sophisticates dancing their way across shipboard ballrooms and promenading along moonlit decks, the men in black tie and tuxedo, the women in designer originals. The movies seldom gave any screen time to the less glamorous events of a ship voyage like seasickness and stormy weather. And while few potential passengers were likely to afford a first class ticket, the media offered relatively little information on the amenities of second or tourist class. The luxury liners were a dream world where discussion of mundane realities seemed highly inappropriate.

Although the great depression of the 1930s would curtail the expansion of the luxury liner fleets, it took the onslaught of World War II to finally end this spectacular era. Non-essential travel was necessarily curtailed or eliminated during the war years, and many liners were requisitioned for military use. After the war, passenger service resumed its popularity, and great liners—including the *United States*, the *France*, and the *Queen Elizabeth II*—continued to be built. But major changes were close at hand. Jet aircraft flights between America and Europe were now available to the public. In 1957, for the first time, the airlines carried a small majority of all transatlantic passengers, and just a few years later the number of people crossing the Atlantic by ship was a mere fraction of the total.

A limited number of liners continued to serve most of their traditional routes, and do so to this day, but veteran ocean travelers knew they had seen the end of an era. The great golden age of the luxury liners—frivolous, extravagant, romantic, and vital—was gone forever.

Chapter One
_T_HE FLOATING PALACES

The story of the great luxury liners begins on a properly epic stage involving heads of state and national rivalries. With most of the world's best passenger vessels, the British had been the leaders of transatlantic shipping for much of the nineteenth century, but toward the end of that century, Germany's Kaiser Wilhelm II became determined to wrest away some of Britain's glory and create for his own country the greatest ship of all time. The North German Lloyd Line built the four-smokestack, 655-foot-long (200 meter) _Kaiser Wilhelm der Grosse_, with a passenger capacity of just under two thousand. The ship was launched in Germany on May 3, 1897, and caused a sensation with the public and all competing shipping lines.

THE GOLDEN AGE BEGINS

Thus began a remarkable era in the annals of shipbuilding, as each of the major companies sought to top the other with the fastest, largest, and most luxurious liners the world had ever seen. The first years of the new century saw the launching of a remarkable series of "superliners"—the Hamburg-America Line's _Deutschland_ (Blue Riband-award-winner for speed, six

years running), North German's _Kronprinz Wilhelm_ and _Kaiser Wilhelm II_, and the White Star Line's _Oceanic_ (completed during the last months of 1899). Suffering from wounded national pride over the Germans' success, the British government subsidized the Cunard Line's building of two gigantic new liners, the _Lusitania_ and the _Mauretania_ (the latter maintaining a record for fastest transatlantic vessel for over two decades). The twin vessels, with their innovative use of steam-turbine engines, quickly regained Britain's pride of place as the country with the fastest and largest liners of the day. Other countries

Opposite: The Hamburg-America Line's _Imperator_, named in honor of Germany's Kaiser Wilhelm II, was ornamented with a gilt figurehead of an eagle clutching a globe in its talons.

Below: A couple enjoys themselves on the deck of the _Deutschland_ in the early years of the twentieth century. The ship carried over two thousand passengers, nearly half of them in steerage.

Left: An illustration from 1929 shows a luxury liner's indoor pool in the smooth, modernist style known as Art Deco. The nautical motifs in Deco luxury liners were copied in land-based designs.

Below: After 1900 the speed and comfort of the great ships made travel for pleasure available to many, and, for the first time, cruises were offered to fabled and exotic lands.

Opposite: A poster for North German Lloyd shows the line's shipping routes. Romanticized, dreamy images like the ones in this poster lured many a first-time passenger to sea.

MAURETANIA AT LANDING STAGE, LIVERPOOL

Above: The *Mauretania* gave Britain an edge in its commercial rivalry with Germany. The ship held the transatlantic speed record from 1907 to 1929, and became the liner most travelers preferred.

Right: A favorite of seasonal travelers, the *Aquitania* was considered by many to be the most beautiful ship afloat.

D. „Kronprinzessin

joined the rivalry, producing their own mammoth vessels such as the Holland-America Line's *Rotterdam* and the French Line's beautifully-appointed *France*, launched in 1912.

The public watched in awe as the rival shipping companies tried to outdo each other with increasingly spectacular results. Cunard's British-based (but American-owned) rival, White Star, produced a trio of transatlantic liners that would be like nothing the world had ever seen. These were given names of unashamed narcissism—the *Gigantic*, the *Olympic*, and the *Titanic*. It seemed hardly possible that anyone could top these colossal creations, but the Germans soon raised the stakes again with the *Imperator*, a staggering 919 feet long (280 meters) and 52,117 gross tons, and a year later, in 1914, the still larger *Vaterland* (later renamed *Leviathan* when seized by the United States), 950 feet in length (290 meters) and 54,282 tons.

The ships were triumphs in more than size. The companies believed these huge structures deserved equally impressive interiors and decorations. Public rooms were now built on an awe-inspiring scale; huge dining and lounging rooms were endowed with decor ranging from high quality to something appropriate for a king's palace. The new ships featured swimming pools, gyms, barber shops, elevators, orchestras, marble pillars, crystal chandeliers, murals, and painted ceilings imitating those of the Sistine Chapel. The deluxe accommodations offered passengers private space on a grand scale as well, with luxuriously furnished multi-room suites.

Ironically, these opulent ships on the busy North Atlantic route earned their greatest profits from the multitudes crammed into the decidedly non-

Above: The beautiful *Kronprinzessin Cecilie* was one of the original German four-stackers, along with the *Kaiser Wilhelm der Grosse*, *Kronprinz Wilhelm*, and *Kaiser Wilhelm II*.

Overleaf: The first of the spectacular French passenger ships, the *France* was commissioned in 1912. The grand and ornately designed first class dining room, seen here, was two decks high, and the cuisine was rated the best available on any luxury liner.

Above: Here we see a portion of the first class lounge on the *Kaiser Wilhelm der Grosse*, the first of the four-stacker liners. The ship's first class rooms displayed the nineteenth-century idea of luxury decor—heavy, plush, and cluttered.

Left: The winter garden on the German ship *Cap Arcona*, which traveled between Germany and South America, was patterned after similar tree-laden interiors in luxury hotels.

Opposite: The grand public rooms of the earliest floating palaces were designed after those in luxury hotels like the Ritz in London. Passengers were meant to forget they were not on land.

Left: Built by Cunard in 1907, the *Lusitania*, like her sister ship *Mauretania*, was a showcase of Edwardian elegance and style.

Below: Smoking rooms such as this on the French liner *Charles Roux* provided a relaxed setting for conversation and cards, but passengers had to be on the lookout for professional gamblers eager to take advantage of inexperienced players.

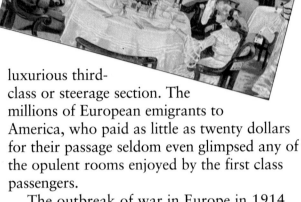

luxurious third-class or steerage section. The millions of European emigrants to America, who paid as little as twenty dollars for their passage seldom even glimpsed any of the opulent rooms enjoyed by the first class passengers.

The outbreak of war in Europe in 1914 brought this first era of the luxury liners to a close. Following the end of World War I, there were great changes in the transatlantic shipping industry. Most of Germany's great liners (including the uncompleted *Bismarck*) would be taken away as war reparations. New laws in America ended the great waves of emigrants crossing the Atlantic by ship, ending much of the profits and the need for ever-larger liners. It would take some time for the companies to regain the momentum of the prewar years, but by the mid-1920s, an even more glorious era was ready to begin.

Above left: For the first years after her launching in 1900, the Hamburg-America Line's *Deutschland* was the world's largest and fastest passenger ship. She was noted for her pleasant public rooms, including the coffee house pictured here.

Above right: The Ritz-Carlton restaurant aboard the German liner *America* was an early effort to offer superior food and service at sea.

Right: Though the immigrant hordes in steerage class far out-numbered the upper classes, they were given a proportionately small amount of open deck space to enjoy. Some steerage passengers slept and ate outdoors, seeking to avoid the illness and lack of sanitation that often plagued the steerage quarters.

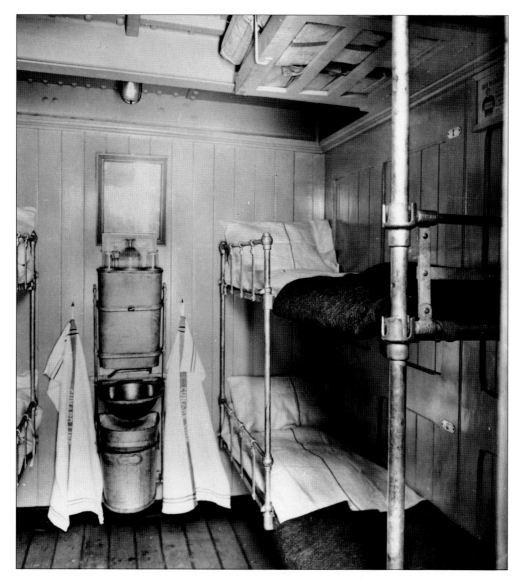

DISASTER AT SEA

The shipping companies did their best to promote their luxury liners as not only the last word in comfort and splendor but, above all, as an extremely safe way to travel. The *Titanic* was promoted to be "unsinkable" (it has been said that the company itself only ever claimed it to be "nearly unsinkable"). Unfortunately, for the image-minded shipping companies, the *Titanic* and her fate would be much better known to the public than all the long-lived liners and thousands of successful transatlantic voyages in all the years to come.

One of the three giant creations of the White Star Line, the *Titanic* was launched on May 31, 1911. In a storm of excited publicity, surrounded by cheering crowds, she left Southampton for New York on her maiden voyage on April 10, 1912. On board were over two thousand passengers and crew. At approximately 11:40 on the night of April 14, the ship's starboard side was sliced open by a huge iceberg. Many of the passengers met the cries to abandon ship with indifference, but confusion and panic increased as the seriousness of the situation became better known. Because of the ship's supposed unsinkability, it was not carrying nearly enough lifeboats to save everyone on board. While some without a place in the boats plunged into the frigid Atlantic, most drowning or freezing to death, others remained on board, stoically facing their doom as the *Titanic* sank

Overleaf: The drama and horrible spectacle of the *Titanic* sinking is captured in this painting by a contemporary artist, Willy Stower. The scene appears well-lit, although the disaster actually took place in the middle of the night.

Above: Lady Duff Gordon, a *Titanic* survivor, was able to escape the sinking ship together with her husband and all of her luggage— 1,500 others were not as fortunate.

Below: A shipboard photo of Mrs. J. Bruce Ismay, a survivor of the *Titanic*. Many survivors met for regular gatherings to remember and reflect on the notorious voyage. In the 1990s a handful of the youngest passengers still survived.

Opposite: The boat deck of the French liner *Paris* shows some of the complex machinery needed to make a great ship run in 1926, but passengers at that time were more likely to appreciate the limitless ocean view.

Right: In New York harbor, passengers and crew members pose for a photograph on the deck of the *Lusitania*. The year is 1908. One of the glories of the Cunard Line, the ship would continue its regal transatlantic run until torpedoed to the bottom of the sea in 1915.

Below: The magnificent *Lusitania* of the Cunard Line, seen in happier times. The ship was a victim of World War I, torpedoed by a German submarine. It sank in under thirty minutes.

Right: Workers view the launching
of the North German Lloyd ship
Bremen. The *Bremen* would soon
take the Blue Riband for the
fastest Atlantic crossing and hold
the title for several years.

Right: Workers view the launching of the North German Lloyd ship *Bremen*. The *Bremen* would soon take the Blue Riband for the fastest Atlantic crossing and hold the title for several years.

into the ocean. The ship's band was said to have remained playing until the tilting of the sinking vessel sent them tumbling into the water. In the end, the disaster took over 1,500 lives.

During World War I, with warships and German U-boats cruising the European coast, passenger liner service across the North Atlantic was kept to the absolute minimum. Cunard's *Lusitania* continued to make round trips between Liverpool, England, and New York, though on a severely reduced schedule. Most passengers who sailed her probably believed the Germans would not attack a ship filled with civilian passengers, but it was later rumored that the *Lusitania* had carried military supplies in her hold.

On the afternoon of May 8, 1915, the *Lusitania* was off the coast of

617. LE HAVRE. Le Paquebot "ILE de FRANCE"

Left: With the launching of the French Line's *Île de France* in 1927, a new standard was set for luxury and aesthetic innovation. For many years the most popular ship on the Atlantic, this majestic vessel remained in service for over thirty years.

Below: A view of the spectacular and legendary first class dining room of the *Île de France*. Over five hundred diners could be seated at one time, and the food was reputed to be the equal of the finest Parisian restaurant.

Ireland and heading home when it was hit with a torpedo. Although—in the wake of the *Titanic* travesty—there were more than enough lifeboats on board, many were rendered unusable as the ship foundered. The liner sank in less than twenty minutes from the time the torpedo hit. A total of 1,198 souls were lost. The death of over one hundred Americans in the sinking was considered a factor in the United States' eventual decision to enter the war.

THE GREAT LADIES

The launch of the *Île de France* in 1927 was the official dawn of the new Golden Age in transatlantic travel. New was the operative word. Inside and out, the *Île de France* represented a breaking away from the past. While previous luxury liners had attempted to approximate the look of landside structures—Renaissance palaces, nineteenth-century grand hotels—and various traditional design elements from the classical to the Baroque, the *Île de France* was entirely original in form and decoration. The inspiration came out of the famed Exposition Internationale des Arts Decoratifs et Industriels Modernes held in Paris in 1925, from which the term Art Deco derived. But it was the *Île*'s stunning application of the new stylistic ideas that put Art Deco on the map. The most innovative and acclaimed new

Above: The *Queen Mary* docks at Southampton. Though not as sleek and advanced as her rival *Normandie*, she was much more popular. The French liner's awesome glamour may have intimidated many passengers.

Opposite: A beautiful and stylish rendering of the North German Lloyd's flagships, *Bremen*, *Columbus*, and *Europa*. Art Deco, the style of this poster, was closely identified with the luxury liners of the 1930s.

Right: Typical of the *Queen Mary*'s Art Deco interior is the first class cocktail bar which features a mural of a carnival.

Below: This watercolor by Albert Sebille of the *Normandie* is titled "Midnight on the Atlantic." The sleek, stylish French liner was considered by many to be the most beautiful ever built.

designers and decorators vied for the chance to add their visions to this flagship for the modern. The dazzling Tea Salon was the work of Ruhlmann, the magnificent modernist glass chandeliers by Lalique, and a huge dining room unlike anything ever put to sea, was the work of the famed Pierre Patout.

The *Ile de France* caused a sensation, particularly among the style conscious and wealthy of the two continents. No members of the trend-following cafe society or other elite groups could consider themselves truly chic without experiencing an Atlantic passage on the dazzling new ship. The other shipping companies took notice: a new standard of excellence had been set. Speed, size, and mere comfort were no longer enough (though speed records would continue to be set and Blue Riband winners would continue to gloat). The new luxury liners would be dreamlike environments, floating pleasure palaces on an epic scale, with no near equivalent on dry land.

Above: One of the stunning works on display in the *Normandie*, Dupas' glass painting *The Chariot of Poseidon* was to be found on the port side of the smoking room. It is now situated in New York's Metropolitan Museum of Art.

While few other countries would ever quite match the aesthetic marvels of the French, an increased attention to style and beauty would be seen in all the great flagships to come. Although many of the great prewar liners had been lost, Germany's new ships would restore her place among the shipping world's giants. North German Lloyd produced the twins *Bremen* and *Europa*, each topping 900 feet (275 meters) in length. They were launched within a day of each other in August of 1928 but the *Europa* caught fire and was held for repairs for another year. This allowed the sister ship to make the first transatlantic run, coming into New York harbor after just four days and sixteen hours, a new world's record. She was awarded the Blue Riband that had been worn for some twenty-two years by the stately veteran ship *Mauretania*. The German ships added a colorful, if short-lived innovation—a small airplane that could be launched from the top deck, carrying mail to the destination ahead from the midway point in the ship's journey.

The Italian Line's magnificent *Rex* and *Conte di Savoia* in part reflected the megalomania of dictator Benito Mussolini, who demanded that Italy have a pair of luxury liners to compare with those of the other Western powers. Traveling the Mediterranean route to New York, the Italian liners emphasized the pleasure of warm weather and sunny skies. The *Rex* featured a huge outdoor swimming pool and sun deck. It was also a speed demon, taking away the *Bremen*'s short-lived glory by winning the Blue Riband in 1933, a year after her first Atlantic crossing.

Not about to be outdone by all the newcomers to the field, Britain produced her greatest superliner, the Cunard's *Queen Mary*. The ship went into service in 1936, and she was a regal presence indeed, with a look that was traditional but with many modernist design elements. Clearly influenced by the Deco-obsessed thirties, the ship was obviously intended to rise above such stylistic trends in favor of a resplendent timelessness. In length, the *Queen Mary* measured a horizon-stretching 1,018 feet (310 meters).

The previous year had seen the first voyages of the French Line's *Normandie*, the largest and arguably the greatest of all luxury liners. She was the unquestioned masterpiece of Streamline Moderne, and a 1,028-foot-long (313-meter), $60 million, spectacular testament to man's industry and imagination. From the size of the rooms to the size of the dinner menu, the *Normandie* sought to vanquish all contenders. Its most lavish suite contained four bedrooms, each with a private bath, a living room the size of a hotel lobby, and a private dining room. Even the most blasé aristocrats and worldliest movie stars were awed by the beauty, spectacle, and perfection of the *Normandie*.

Alas, her reign as the queen of the seas was short and its end tragic. By 1939, with a war starting in Europe, and after only four years in operation, the *Normandie* was ordered to stay in New York harbor for safekeeping. After the surrender of France to Hitler, the ship was seized by the United States government. A fire and then flooding left her capsized in port. Huge crowds gathered to watch the laborious attempts to raise her, but it could not be done and the ship was ultimately sold for scrap.

Like the other superliners, the *Normandie*'s grand scale made it nearly impossible for her to make a profit. She and the others were aided by government subsidization for their roles as glittering symbols of national pride and strength. The war made such matters irrelevant. Many of the liners were unceremoniously seized for use as troopships; others were torn apart for needed scrap metal. However well made and well intentioned, the postwar passenger ships would never attain the special quality of the great floating palaces of the past.

Above: Titled "Sports," this witty lacquer panel was one of four created by Jean Dunand for the *Normandie*'s smoking room. The classical Greek image of javelin, weight, and discus throwers is made contemporary with 1930s swimsuits and hairstyles.

Below: This colorful cross-sectional view of the *Normandie* shows the incredible complexity and diversity of the ship's interior.

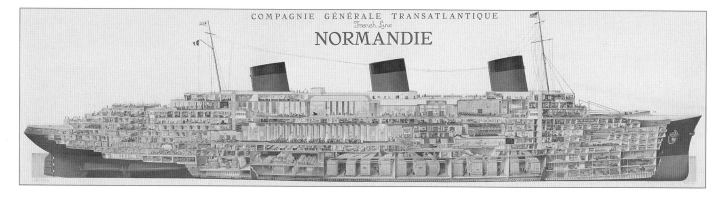

COMPAGNIE GÉNÉRALE TRANSATLANTIQUE
French Line
NORMANDIE

Chapter Two
LIFE ABOARD SHIP

Opposite: The French Line sailed the Atlantic, Pacific, and Mediterranean. Pleasure cruises became vital to shipping lines in the 1930s since transatlantic business had been sharply affected by the Great Depression.

For today's traveler crossing an ocean by air, the journey usually begins with a frantic ride to the airport, followed by delays, long lines, uncertainty, and, finally, a confining seat and a mediocre meal. The prewar traveler by luxury liner, on the other hand, began their trip abroad in high spirits, often surrounded by family and friends, not to mention champagne and bon voyage presents. The entire vessel would likely be in a carnival-like mood for hours before the first signal that departure was imminent. No matter how regular transoceanic service had become, the departure of one of the famed luxury liners was always a special event.

Below: Though ocean crossings were routine, the departure of a great liner was always a special event at which friends and family gathered to wish travelers a safe and happy voyage.

DEPARTURE—
THE FIRST DAY AT SEA

In New York City, the area around a departing liner became a chaos of honking cars and taxis, acres of suitcases and giant metal trunks, police, customs agents, longshoremen, and crowds of passengers and well-wishers that could number in the thousands.

On board, ship chaos reigned equally supreme, with the ship's staff trying vainly to do their duty. Staterooms and suites would be packed to overflowing with visitors, champagne corks popping all about, toasts raised to a happy voyage, and portable record players turned to full volume as the revelers danced between bundles of flowers and gift-wrapped fruit baskets.

Manhattan's elite considered midnight sailings to be particularly chic (though late-night departures were merely for the practical purpose of a

Right: A sporty touring car being loaded aboard ship. In the heyday of the luxury liners, the "idle rich" might be abroad on holiday for months at a time. Passengers brought along numerous huge steamer trunks, and, if it was deemed convenient, could ship a favorite automobile as well.

Above: The staff of the *Normandie* poses for a rare group portrait. From the captain of the ship to the humblest cabin boy, the ship carried in its employ nearly thirteen hundred men and women, of whom only about one-half are shown here.

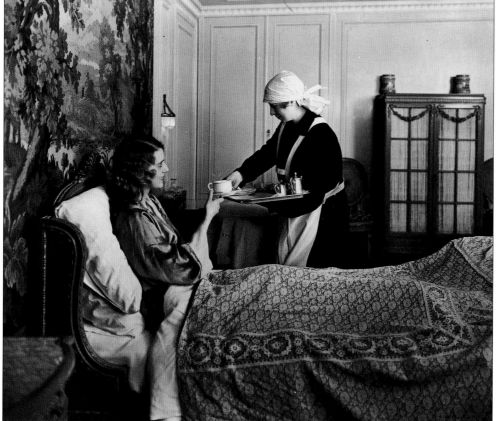

Left: A passenger enjoys breakfast in bed in the deluxe "Miramar" suite on the *Saturnia*. The large suites on a luxury liner might contain as many rooms as a penthouse apartment, with a full staff of servants to take care of every need.

Right: A waiter, in appropriate garb, prepares a tray in the Moorish tea room on the *France*. Decorated from floor to ceiling to resemble a corner of Algiers or Marrakech, the room reflected France's colonial rule in North Africa.

morning arrival in France). Passengers and entourage, all in their finest evening clothes, would leave their favorite restaurant or nightclub to swarm aboard ship and continue a farewell party. Sometimes a band would be playing on the ship and dozens of couples would swirl around the dance floor. At last, moving amid the noise and confusion, uniformed stewards would signal that departure time was at hand, banging a small gong or ringing chimes and shouting the time-tested phrase, "All ashore that's going ashore!" Stragglers would finally be stirred by the ship's mighty whistle, a heart-stopping sound that could be heard for miles.

The chaos of the visitors would now be replaced by the regimented activity of the crew. Passengers stood on deck to wave to friends on the pier, or else explored their rooms, did some unpacking or, if too much champagne had been drunk, simply collapsed on their beds and slept. Slowly the ship would start to move and the city skyline would begin to diminish; the Atlantic lay just ahead . . . the voyage had begun.

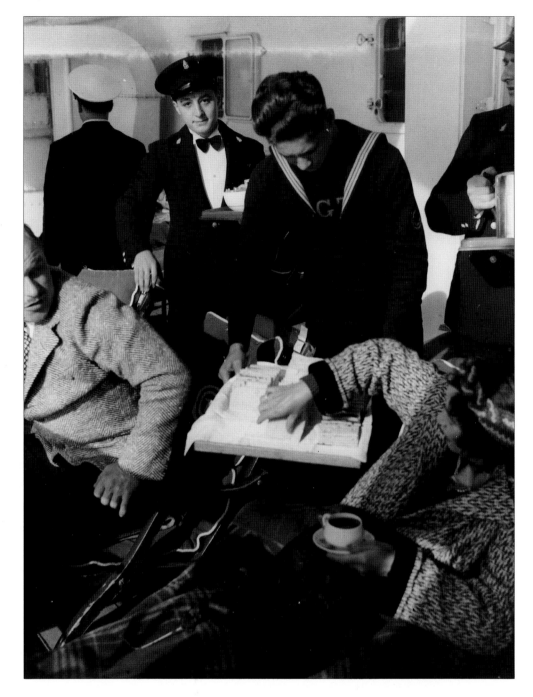

Luxury liners were famed for both the quality and the quantity of their staffs. In the prewar years, the number of stewards, bellboys, and other serving staff on board was such that every first class passenger was able to feel that he or she had their own personal servants. Those who were regular voyagers on a ship would have favorite stewards who knew their special needs. Barmen and dining room stewards tried to remember the drink of choice of regular passengers. The goal of an attentive steward was, of course, a good tip at the end of a voyage. While their salaries were modest, gratuities gave many stewards a much higher income than that of the ship's captain. Snobbery might have been rampant among first class passengers, but it could not compare with the disdain of a steward for a passenger who tipped poorly or not at all.

On the first day at sea, passengers would need to take care of matters like deck chair placement and seating in the dining room. The more generous passengers found the most desirable places for enjoying the fresh air on

Right: This fanciful poster for the
Cunard Line is one of many eagerly
sought today by enthusiasts of
maritime memorabilia and the
graphic arts.

deck in the unavoidable wooden foldout chairs. The sea air could be
bracing and stewards would help secure the passenger within a warm
woolen blanket, and bring hot tea and soup.

Many passengers found it imperative to secure the right seating for
dinner. The place of honor was at the Captain's table. It was not considered
proper to actually request a place with the Captain, though many did. The
passenger list would be combed for appropriate honorees, and naturally,

Right: The rotunda of the *France* was typical of the ship's palatial public rooms. The much admired decor was largely in the style of Louis XIV, though there were other design influences as well, including the Moorish tea room.

Left: French luxury liners were renowned for their distinctive and beautiful interiors. Pictured here is the grand staircase and foyer of the *Paris*, the first of the French Line's series of great ships following World War I.

Right: Ships' smoking rooms were originally considered to be "for men only." The spirit of this outmoded custom was retained in the determinedly masculine decor for the smoking room of the *Washington*—a ship of the United States Line. Fashioned to resemble a woodsy, if sophisticated, hunting lodge, the bison and moose heads and the paintings of Native Americas also reflected the ship's heritage.

Below: Illustrations such as this, which depicts a spectacular grand salon, showed first class travel as the exclusive domain of the rich and the super-chic.

any celebrities on board would be given a high priority. However, this could sometimes be problematic if the celebrity roster included ex-lovers or a pair of feuding rivals. The Captain's staff was expected to keep up with gossip to avoid any embarrassing scenes.

Though movie stars and other famous faces were common on the North Atlantic liners, they were hardly treated like common passengers. Stewards had to be aware of when a star was being pestered by unwanted attentions and hurry to their rescue. Liner travel was considered to be conducive to romance and many marriage-minded women and mothers with daughters would book passage on a liner that would be carrying an eligible millionaire or movie star. Some celebrities, most notably Greta Garbo, with her legendary avoidance of public attention, would spend an entire transatlantic voyage locked in their suites.

TOURING THE
GREAT PUBLIC ROOMS

The popularity of the giant flagships was certainly due in part to the fact that they were the fastest on the ocean routes, and their size and superior stabilizers guaranteed a quieter and much more comfortable journey. But it was easy to forget about these practical matters when surrounded by the spectacle and opulence of a luxury liner's architecture and decor.

Below: The grand lounge of the *Normandie* was two and a half decks high—comparable in size and proportion to the Hall of Mirrors at Versailles.

Above: Whether called a music room or winter garden, public rooms of this kind, filled with sunlight and tropical plants, were favorite meeting places for afternoon tea at sea.

Right: This menu for a 1914 dinner aboard the *Lusitania* is written in an amalgam of French and English. Many passengers kept their menus as souvenirs, and today these are highly prized by collectors.

R.M.S. "LUSITANIA"   SUNDAY, SEPTEMBER 13, 1914

Menu

Tortue Verte   Crème Chatrillon

Supreme de Sole—Palace

Mousse de Jambon—Alexandra

Sirloin & Ribs of Beef

Green Peas   Rice   Cauliflower à la Crème
Boiled, Mashed & Chateau Potatoes

Chapon—Chipolata

Salade de Saison

Pouding Saxone   Petits Fours

Gâteau Mexicaine

Bavarois au Chocolat

Ices   Café

Dessert

CUNARD LINE

As the pride of their lines, the luxury liners were scrupulously maintained, scrubbed, and polished to a gleaming finish. No expense was spared in the materials used and the attention to detail. World-renowned architects, artists, and interior designers were employed to make each great liner a unique and dazzling work of art. Everywhere passengers were surrounded by paintings, sculpture, intricate craftsmanship, carved glass, smooth marble, and spotless chrome.

At the start of the luxury liner boom in the 1920s, most ships maintained a traditional or classic look in their design and decoration, a plush, ornate nineteenth-century style. The French were the first to embrace the fresh, forward-looking ideas of Art Deco, in the *Île de France* and later with the *Normandie*. Other liners followed the trend— designer Brian O'Rourke's *Orion* for the British

Orient Line (serving Australia and Asian ports) was a chrome and curvilinear masterwork of almost futuristic appeal. The Netherlands' pride and joy, the *Nieuw Amsterdam*, was another innovative representative of modernist, streamlined design. The Cunard Line hedged its bet with the magnificent *Queen Mary*, christened in 1934 by the British monarch, allowing only a restrained use of Art-Deco motifs. Still other new liners went their own way stylistically, as with the Italian Line's *Conte di Savoia*, which offered public halls of marble and gold leaf and an ethereal painted ceiling, all as if directly taken from a Renaissance palazzo. The *Johan Van Oldenbarnevelt*, a Dutch liner that carried 770 passengers to the Dutch East Indies, reflected its Asian destination with a riot of chinoiserie, bamboo, teak, and other Oriental elements.

A ship's features were

Above: With the new wave of "floating palaces" built in the 1920s and 1930s, designers envisioned ever more impressive public rooms such as this rendering of a first class dining room.

Left: This tempting meal was served on Thanksgiving aboard the *President Wilson*, en route to Yokahama, Japan. On the long voyage across the Pacific, large and frequent meals were an important way of passing the time.

Above: Passengers danced to live music of the late 1920s in the *Vulcania*'s magnificently decorated ballroom. This Italian liner eschewed the sleek lines of the new Art Deco style for ornate glitter reminiscent of the Baroque.

Below: A glimpse of the busy kitchen staff on board the French liner *Lafayette*. Preparing three major meals, as well as snacks, teas, and assorted extras for up to a thousand passengers kept a ship's kitchen in nearly constant commotion.

Above: The pastry chef of the *S.S. Berengaria*, Luigi Camano (left) is seen here admiring one of his spectacular creations, a cake topped with a miniature Eiffel Tower. On board the great liners, desserts were often the province of a separate kitchen staff.

Opposite: The first class dining room of the *Normandie* could seat seven hundred diners with ease. Measuring 282 feet in length (82 meters), its gold interior was lit by twelve massive Lalique light towers placed at intervals throughout the room.

designed both to distract and to dazzle. The furnishings, windows, and other accoutrements in the major public rooms were designed to let the passengers forget that they were aboard a vessel in the middle of an ocean. These rooms could as easily have been within some grand hotel, palace, or country estate. Conceivably, a passenger could dress for dinner in his suite, make his way to the dining room, and then on to the smoking room for a cigar, coffee, or after dinner drink—all without ever noticing that he was surrounded by an ocean.

It is difficult for anyone who was never aboard a giant luxury liner to imagine the colossal scale of the large public rooms. The Art-Nouveau foyer and double-sided staircase on the original *France*, for instance, would not have looked out of place at a major opera house. Grand staircases were a feature of some dining rooms so that the fancily-dressed passengers could make a suitably noticeable entrance. The dining rooms of the *Manhattan* and the *Reliance* were overlooked by a curtained balcony where an orchestra discreetly serenaded the diners. Some ships had winter gardens patterned after those in deluxe hotels, huge rooms for socializing that approximated an outdoor environment with high ceilings, potted trees, and plants. The so-called smoking rooms on liners were popular places for a relaxed drink and a cigar—masculine enclaves in the beginning, they were eventually liberated for use by both genders. Most were good-sized but cozy rooms, though not all—the one on the *Conte Grande*, was an ornate extravaganza that combined the

Above: Aboard the *Aquitania*, a posed publicity photo shows Walter Hagen giving tips on the proper golf swing to Helen McKellar and Madge Kennedy, stage stars of the 1920s. The invariable presence of celebrities was one of the allures of luxury liner travel.

Opposite: The climax of every voyage was a gala evening that included dancing and special entertainment, but the real spectacle was provided by the passengers themselves, arrayed in their finest clothes and jewelry.

Baroque with elements out of the *Arabian Nights*.

First class staterooms and suites were equally elaborate and impressive. A suite might include a living room, dressing room, one or two large bedrooms, a full bathroom with tub, and perhaps an outdoor verandah with tables and lounge chairs. Decor reflected the style of the public rooms, whether that was Louis XIV or Streamline Moderne. Under the assumption that visibly nautical elements were déclassé, the deluxe suites replaced portholes with windows and eliminated bunks in favor of conventional beds.

Above: Passengers take part in a sack race on the deck of a liner in 1900. Depending on the line and its social directors, some passenger ships provided an almost non-stop series of games and organized events.

Left: On the deck of the *Bermuda* a female passenger boxes an upright dummy under the watchful eye of the ship's athletic coach. A wide variety of sporting and athletic activities were available on all liners.

PASSING THE TIME AWAY

With passengers on board ship for nearly a week on transatlantic crossings (and considerably more to cross the Pacific or on round-the-world journeys) the shipping companies knew they had to provide their customers with more than mere transportation. Indeed, most of the public rooms and facilities on a liner were there to preoccupy the passengers and make them forget they were at sea, however comfortably, for the duration of the voyage.

Taking care of some hours each day, of course, was the elaborate meal

Opposite: A group of sophisticated transatlantic voyagers take in a game of deck tennis. Beginning in the 1920s, the new liners provided more open deck space for first class passengers.

Right: Swimming pools, a rarity before World War I, became increasingly common on liners of the 1920s and 1930s. Italian liners, following the warmer southern Atlantic route, had outdoor pools.

service. In addition to breakfast and lunch in the daytime there was always the possibility of hot bouillon while lounging in a deck chair, and, on British ships, full tea service in the afternoon. Dinner was a considerably more formal event, as the dining room was one of the showpieces of most liners. The strikingly modernistic first-class dining room on the *Île de France* could seat over five hundred at a time. The dazzling dining room on the later *Normandie* doubled that capacity. A huge bronze entranceway led into the awe-inspiring environment, which was "larger than the Hall of Mirrors at Versailles," or so the publicists said. In these rooms passengers dined on elaborate, multi-course meals. The French ships, not too surprisingly, were known to have the best chefs.

Drinking was a popular pastime in the ships' bars and nightclubs. Throughout the 1920s, until the repeal of Prohibition in 1933, the bars were particularly popular with thirsty American passengers. Wagering and games of chance were a distraction for others. There was always the ship's pool, where passengers wagered on the ship's mileage or exact time of arrival. Cards were played in the smoking rooms or, when the games became more serious, in someone's suite. Professional gamblers and cheats were a perennial problem on the Atlantic route, zeroing in on rich and naive targets and fleecing them for enormous sums.

For some, sea travel was conducive to exercise. In the morning, the promenade deck would see a steady stream of fast-walking passengers circumnavigating the ship. Many ships had Olympic-sized swimming pools, almost always filled with salt water. Ships designed for the North Atlantic generally had indoor pools, but those on the sunnier Mediterranean route, like the Italian liners, could have them outdoors and offer more open deck space for sunbathing. The German *Imperator* had a remarkable marble and tile "Pompeian Bath" fit for a Roman emperor. The athletically-minded could also usually find a well-stocked gymnasium, while sporting types might enjoy golfing, skeet shooting, tennis, shuffleboard, or other "deck sports." The *Paris* had a croquet court while the *France* had an outdoor bowling alley. For those not seduced by even the more sedate sort of athletics, there were well-stocked libraries, complete with plush armchairs, and writing rooms for jotting letters or starting one's memoirs. Movies were shown on most ships, usually in improvised screening rooms; the *Normandie* was the first ship to have her own movie theater.

In addition to these and other activities and distractions, ships held dances, recitals, fancy dress balls, and masquerades. For those passengers who did not learn to pace themselves, an ocean voyage could be a very exhausting experience.

Above: The aft sundeck on any ship was a favorite spot for games, sunbathing, and people watching. Often equipped with an outdoor pool, it was particularly pleasant along the southern ocean routes.

Chapter Three
MYTH, MEDIA & POPULAR CULTURE

Opposite: A round-the-world cruise was certainly a tempting prospect for the dedicated traveler. In this magazine illustration from 1911, passengers in an Eastern port are offered exotic fruits by local vendors.

Overleaf: Nattily dressed onlookers watch passengers board the French ship *Massilia* in this painting from the 1920s.

Below: Dockside at Le Havre, these two smartly dressed French-women stand beside their nation's pride and joy, the *Normandie*. The ship was considered the epitome of style and chic.

*N*o matter how many ocean-going ships were built or how relatively inexpensive a third class ticket, only a tiny percentage of all potential passengers would ever actually experience a voyage on a luxury liner. In the days before jets and package tours, even the third class passenger had to have two weeks free just for the transatlantic passage and return.

THE ALLURE OF THE LINERS

Aside from the wealthy—some of whom crisscrossed the ocean as if it were a commute from the suburbs—the passengers on the North Atlantic runs included many vacationing college students and teachers with the entire summer off, as well as retirees enjoying "the trip of a lifetime." The average working person in prewar America or Europe would have been no more likely to go on a pleasure trip aboard a floating palace than they would a trip to the moon.

The appeal of a first class transatlantic passage on a great ocean liner, however, extended to far beyond those relative few who would actually experience it first hand. To many who lived near the waterways or ports of call of the liners, merely seeing the mighty vessels was cause for excitement. Children—and many adults—would stand for hours waiting for a ship's arrival or to watch it pull out to sea. Federico Fellini's *Amarcord* recreates a lyrical scene from his childhood, the villagers of all ages elatedly gathering together for a brief but unforgettable glimpse of a passing ship of the glorious Italian Line.

On the day of a liner's departure

Speisehaus der olympischen Kämpfer

BREMEN

EUROPA

NORD LLOYD

80

JAHRE	YEARS
Erfahrung in Betreuung und Verpflegung	of experience in catering and provisioning

Lloyd-Stewards und *Lloyd-Köche* betreuen und verpflegen auch die olympischen Kämpfer im Olympischen Dorf

Lloyd stewards, Lloyd chefs to wait on, to provide for competitors in Olympic village

NORDDEUTSCHER LLOYD BREMEN

from port, many fans of the luxury ships would permit themselves a closer inspection. Taking advantage of the crowds and confusion at such times, with endless visitors flocking back and forth and filling the passageways, some determined young people would slip aboard for a surreptitious tour. A few would so fall under the spell of a ship's magnificence that they would decide not to leave at the last call. Most stowaways were found by the crew in time to transship them to a pilot boat and a quick return to port. Legal charges were seldom filed as the crews understood the siren call of a great ship.

LINERS AND THE MEDIA

It was hard not to be aware of the comings and goings of the major passenger ships. Most newspapers contained a daily listing of all departures and arrivals, and armchair travelers could savor the legendary ships' names and their glamorous or exotic destinations.

Advertisements for the luxury liners could be found in the higher-toned papers and Sunday supplements as well as glossy travel magazines. Assorted shipping companies created colorful enticements to come aboard their fabulous liners. Above a drawing of the Taj Mahal and its reflective pools a 1929 advertisement asked "Sailing East to Suez?" and below, there was a ready answer: "Then of course P&O . . ."—meaning a voyage on a liner of the Peninsular and Oriental Company. Though not ignoring the romance inherent in a glimpse of the Taj Mahal, the advertisement was

Above left: Evoking an image of sophistication and style long associated with ocean travel, this poster for the Cunard Line plays upon the desire of the prospective traveler to dine lavishly in the company of the wealthy international set.

Above right: Two legendary modes of travel, the luxury liner and the express train, are combined in this poster by Albert Sebille for the French Line and the French State Railway.

Opposite: Colorful magazine advertisements, as well as those hanging in travel agency windows, made the names of the great shipping companies and their vessels well known to the public.

Right: This looming, smoothly curving rendition of the *Normandie* by artist A. M. Cassandre is the most famous of all ocean liner posters. It remains one of the most emblematic graphic posters of the 1930s.

aimed primarily at the practical traveler—colonists from the British empire—and emphasized speed and efficiency (with just a bit of racial chauvinism thrown in for good measure):

To sojourners in India, explorers, pleasure-bound world travelers . . . from Suez east to Kobe, from Bombay south to Sydney . . . P&O is

Opposite top: Posing for a publicity photo on board Italy's *Conte Biancamano* are the king and queen of the silent cinema, Douglas Fairbanks and Mary Pickford, together with their adopted daughter. Shipping lines took every opportunity to publicize the patronage of Hollywood stars.

Opposite below: On the aft sundeck of the *Queen Mary* Jesse Owens is welcomed home in August of 1936 by a crowd of dignitaries, reporters, and newsreel cameramen. The athlete (bottom center) had recently broken track records and won three gold medals at the Olympic games in Berlin.

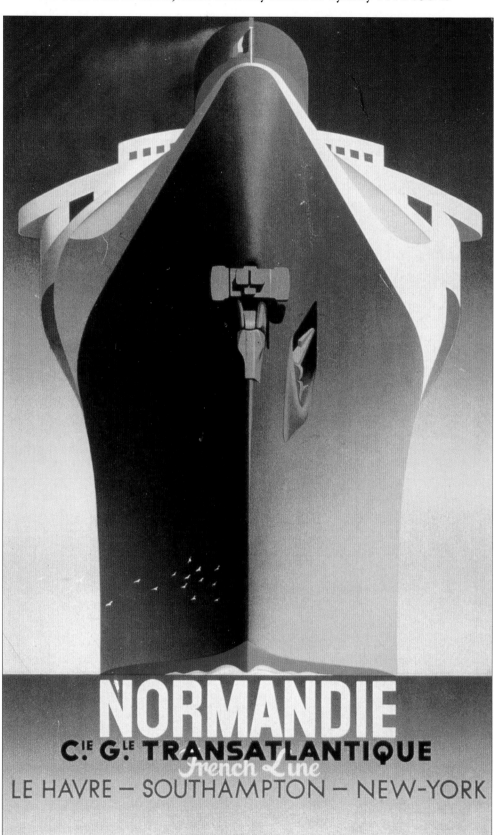

traditionally the link with their homeland and the route to anywhere. Swift and sure, punctual in their arrival, these Liners are to Indians symbolical of the might and splendour of the West! When business or pleasure calls you East of Suez, take this route—preferred for safety and luxurious comfort since 1840.

For cruises, where time mattered not at all and the potential passengers did not need to be reminded of their "superiority," the advertisements emphasized pleasure, bright colors, and comfort—in short, the best of everything. An advertisement for a world cruise by the Red Star Line's *Belgenland* trumpeted:

> The largest, finest liner that has ever circled the globe! Sail Westward from New York Dec. 20 on a gorgeous, 133-day itinerary . . . a lifetime of exciting sensations in 19 vivid weeks. Sample the flavor of the world's most glamorous cities, each at a delectable season—with arrival in Europe in April for Spring sojourns!

Above: In an extraordinary spectacle photographed on September 9, 1934, the liner *Morro Castle* is seen lying grounded and on fire just before the public beach at Asbury Park, New Jersey. Only a few hours from New York when disaster struck, the *Morro Castle* fire took over one hundred lives.

A forty-six-day cruise to the Mediterranean aboard the White Star Line's *S.S. Adriatic* implored the reader to "Revel in old-world charm and twentieth-century sophistication . . . the hoary antiquity of Egypt, the savoir faire of Monte Carlo!"

One didn't have to open a newspaper or magazine to be lured by the liner companies. The better travel agencies were bound to be full of extravagant posters featuring vividly colored, almost dreamlike artists' renderings of the ships. Some poster paintings, like A. M. Cassandre's almost abstract rendering of the *Normandie*, were hailed as works of fine modern art.

Free publicity for the shipping lines was regularly provided in the media, particularly the newsreels. (A newsreel was a twelve-minute journalistic potpourri shown in movie theaters before the featured film.) Any time a new liner was to be launched a regal ceremony was usually held, with a celebrity christening the ship by sending a giant bottle of champagne crashing against the hull; the newsreel cameras were sure to be there to record it.

Camera crews and reporters and emissaries from the tabloid newspapers regularly swarmed aboard a transatlantic liner on its arrival in search of

Right: The publicity generated by celebrity passengers added luster to the reputations of the ships on which they sailed. Here, silent screen idol Rudolph Valentino arrives in New York with his wife after a holiday abroad in 1924.

Overleaf left: The sinking of the *Titanic* produced a media frenzy. In New York, crowds surged around the newspaper offices to learn the latest telegraphed details of the disaster. The tragic story made headlines for weeks. Seen here, the April 16, 1912 issue of *The New York Times* devoted the entire front page and most of the other pages to *Titanic* coverage.

Overleaf right: Shipwrecks have always held a morbid fascination in the public eye. The 1906 collision of the *Orinoco* and the *Kaiser Wilhelm der Grosse* was vividly depicted in a French periodical of the day.

The New York Times.

VOL. LXI...NO. 19,906. NEW YORK, TUESDAY, APRIL 16, 1912.—TWENTY-FOUR PAGES. ONE CENT In Greater New York | Elsewhere TWO CENTS

TITANIC SINKS FOUR HOURS AFTER HITTING ICEBERG; 866 RESCUED BY CARPATHIA, PROBABLY 1250 PERISH; ISMAY SAFE, MRS. ASTOR MAYBE, NOTED NAMES MISSING

Col. Astor and Bride, Isidor Straus and Wife, and Maj. Butt Aboard.

"RULE OF SEA" FOLLOWED

Women and Children Put Over in Lifeboats and Are Supposed to be Safe on Carpathia.

PICKED UP AFTER 8 HOURS

Vincent Astor Calls at White Star Office for News of His Father and Leaves Weeping.

FRANKLIN HOPEFUL ALL DAY

Manager of the Line Insisted Titanic Was Unsinkable Even After She Had Gone Down.

HEAD OF THE LINE ABOARD

J. Bruce Ismay Making First Trip on Gigantic Ship That Was To Surpass All Others.

The Lost Titanic Being Towed Out of Belfast Harbor.

CAPT. E. J. SMITH,
Commander of the Titanic.

Biggest Liner Plunges to the Bottom at 2:20 A. M.

RESCUERS THERE TOO LATE

Except to Pick Up the Few Hundreds Who Took to the Lifeboats.

WOMEN AND CHILDREN FIRST

Cunarder Carpathia Rushing to New York with the Survivors.

SEA SEARCH FOR OTHERS

The Californian Stands By on Chance of Picking Up Other Boats or Rafts.

OLYMPIC SENDS THE NEWS

Only Ship to Flash Wireless Message to Shore After the Disaster.

LATER REPORT SAVES 866.

BOSTON, April 15.—A wireless message picked up late to-night, relayed from the Olympic, says that the Carpathia is on her way to New York with 866 passengers from the steamer Titanic aboard. They are mostly women and children, the message said, and it concluded: "Grave fears are felt for the safety of the balance of the passengers and crew."

PARTIAL LIST OF THE SAVED.

Includes Bruce Ismay, Mrs. Widener, Mrs. H. B. Harris, and an incomplete name, suggesting Mrs. Astor's.

Special to The New York Times.

CAPE RACE, N. F., Tuesday, April 16.—Following is a partial list of survivors among the first-class passengers of the Titanic, received by the Marconi wireless station this morning from the Carpathia, via the steamship Olympic:

Mr. JACOB P. —— and maid.
Mr. HARRY ANDERSON.
Mr. ED. W. APPLETON.
Mrs. ROSE ABBOTT.
Miss G. M. BURNS.
Miss D. D. CASSEBERE.
Mrs. WM. M. CLARKE.
Mrs. B. CHIBINACE.
Miss E. G. CROSSBIE.
Miss H. ROSEBIE.
Miss JEAN HIPACK.
Mrs. HY. B. HARRIS.
Mrs. ALEX. HALVERSON.
Mrs. MARGARET BAYS.
Mr. BRUCE ISMAY.
Mr. and Mrs. ED. KIMBERLEY.
Mr. F. A. KENNYMAN.
Miss EMILE KENCHEN.
Miss G. F. LONGLEY.
Mr. A. F. LEADER.
Miss BERTHA LAVORY.
Miss ERNEST LIVER.
Miss MARY CLINES.
Miss SINGRID LINDSTROM.
Mr. GUSTAVE J. LESNEUR.
Miss GIORGETTA A. MADILL.
Mrs. MELICARD.
Mrs. TUCKER and maid.
Mrs. J. B. THAYER.
Mr. J. B. THAYER, Jr.
Mr. HENRY WOOLMER.
Miss ANNA WARD.
Mr. RICHARD M. WILLIAMS.
Mrs. F. M. WARNER.
Mrs. HELEN A. WILSON.
Miss WILLARD.
Miss MARY WICKS.
Mr. GEO. D. WIDENER and maid.
Mr. J. STEWART WHITE.
Miss MARIE YOUNG.
Mr. THOMAS POTTER, Jr.
Mrs. EDNA S. ROBERTS.

Mr. C. ROLMANE.
Mrs. SUSAN P. ROGERSON. (Prob. Ryerson).
Miss EMILY B. ROGERSON.
Mrs. ARTHUR ROGERSON.
Master ALLISON and nurse.
Miss K. T. ANDREWS.
Miss NINETTE PANHART.
Miss E. W. ALLEN.
Mr. and Mrs. D. BISHOP.
Mr. H. BLANK.
Miss A. BASSINA.
Mr. JAMES BAXTER.
Mr. GEORGE A. BATT.
Mrs. C. BONNELL.
Mrs. J. M. BROWN.
Miss G. C. BOWEN.
Mr. and Mrs. R. L. BECK.
Miss RUTH TAUSSIG.
Miss ELLA THOR.
Mr. and Mrs. E. Z. TAYLOR.
GILBERT M. TUCKER.
Mr. R. B. THAYER.
Mr. JOHN B. ROGERSON.
Mrs. M. ROTHSCHILD.
Miss MADELEINE NEWELL.
Miss MARJORIE NEWELL.
HELEN W. NEWSOM.
Mr. FIENNAD OMOND.
Mr. E. C. OSTBY.
Miss HELEN R. OSTBY.
Mr. MAMAM J. RENAGO.
Mlle. OLIVIA.
Mrs. D. W. MERVIN.
Mr. PHILIP EMOCK.
Mr. JAMES GOOGHT.
Miss RUBERTA MAIMY.
Mr. PIERRE MARECHAL.
Mr. W. E. MINEHAN.
Miss APPIE BANELT.
Major ARTUR PEUCHEN.
Mrs. KARL H. BEHR.
Miss DESSETTE.

Mrs. WILLIAM BUCKNELL.
Mrs. O. H. BARKWORTH.
Mrs. H. B. STEFFASON.
Mrs. ELSIE BOWERMAN.

The Marconi station reports that it missed the word after "Mrs. Jacob P." In a list received by the Associated Press this morning this name appeared well down, but in THE TIMES list it is first, suggesting that the name of Mrs. John Jacob Astor is intended. This supposition is strengthened by the fact that, except for Mrs. H. J. Allison, Mrs. Astor is the only lady in the "A" column of the ship's passenger list attended by a maid.

NAMES PICKED UP AT BOSTON.

BOSTON, April 15.—Among the names of survivors of the Titanic picked up by wireless from the steamer Carpathia here to-night were the following:

Mr. and Mrs. L. HENRY.
Mrs. W. A. HOOPER.
Mr. MILE.
Mr. J. FLYNN.
Miss ALICE FORTUNE.
Mr. ROBERT DOUGLAS.
Miss HILDA SLAYTER.
Mrs. P. SMITH.
Mrs. BRAHAM.
Miss LUCILLE CARTER.
Mr. WILLIAM CARTER.
Miss CUMMINGS.
Mrs. FLORENCE MARE.
Miss ALICE PHILLIPS.
Mrs. PAULA MUNGE.
Mrs. JANE.
Mrs. PHYLLIS G.
HOWARD B. CASE.
Miss MINEHAN.
Miss BERTHA.

Dix Huitième année. — N° 931.　　Huit pages : CINQ centimes　　Dimanche 9 Décembre 1906.

Le Petit Parisien

SUPPLÉMENT LITTÉRAIRE ILLUSTRÉ

TOUS LES JOURS
Le Petit Parisien
(Six pages)
5 centimes

CHAQUE SEMAINE
LE SUPPLÉMENT LITTÉRAIRE
5 centimes

DIRECTION: 18, rue d'Enghien (10e), PARIS

ABONNEMENTS
—
PARIS ET DÉPARTEMENTS :
12 mois, 4 fr. 50. 6 mois, 2 fr. 25.
UNION POSTALE :
12 mois, 5 fr. 50. 6 mois, 3 fr.

EN RADE DE CHERBOURG

Above: Outside the London headquarters of the White Star Line a newsboy sells accounts of the tragedy that stunned the world.

Opposite: The public fascination with great liners in distress produced such strange artifacts as this French jigsaw puzzle showing the sinking of the *Lusitania*.

celebrity interviews. A line's publicity office might leak word that Charlie Chaplin and Paulette Goddard, for instance, would be aboard the *Queen Mary* when it docked in New York. The Hollywood stars or other famous names could usually be persuaded to hold a brief press conference on deck.

Some press coverage was far from positive but inevitable. A disaster at sea involving a luxury liner was a major media event and might inspire daily headlines and feature stories for weeks, along with cartoons, editorials, and commemorative poems. With the size of the vessels and the number of passengers aboard, any liner disaster held the possibility of visual spectacle as well as massive human tragedy.

When news of the *Titanic*'s sinking reached New York, huge crowds gathered outside the office buildings of the Manhattan newspapers, anxiously awaiting the latest reports. As the rescue ship *Carpathia* came into New York harbor it was surrounded by chartered tugboats filled beyond capacity with journalists. And later, when the *Titanic* survivors began disembarking, the newspaper photographers' flash flares lit up the sky.

The sinking of the *Lusitania* and the disastrous fire aboard the *Morro Castle* in 1934 (taking over one hundred lives with the ship only a few hours away from New York) were among the other luxury liner tragedies that received maximum press coverage and came to be remembered by almost everyone who lived at the time. Conversely, the lack of extended press coverage of the sinking of the Canadian Pacific's Liverpool to Quebec passenger ship *Empress of Ireland*, with 1,024 lives lost (the second worst shipping disaster in history) kept the ship from attaining the mythic status of other doomed liners.

FRED GINGER
ASTAIRE ROGERS
"SHALL WE DANCE"
with
EDWARD EVERETT HORTON · ERIC BLORE · JEROME COWAN
KETTI GALLIAN · WILLIAM BRISBANE and HARRIET HOCTOR

Above: For the average person in the 1930s, the years of the Great Depression, viewing shipboard scenes in films like *Shall We Dance?* was as close as they were likely to get to a dazzling first class crossing.

BOOKS AND MOVIES

Popular culture of the period did much to make the public familiar with life aboard a luxury liner. Globetrotting novelists and playwrights commuting between the London and New York stages, were regular customers for the passenger lines (Noel Coward penned his *Private Lives* during a transpacific cruise), and naturally put their experiences to good use in books and plays set aboard ships.

Comic novelist P. G. Wodehouse, whose uproarious stories dealt with the most indolent of leisure class Englishmen, set many of his characters loose among the first class cabins and lounges of the great Atlantic liners. Somerset Maugham, in stories like "Mr Knowall," conveyed the milieu of luxury cruisers and ocean crossings with the incidental details of one who knew these things from experience. In fact, Maugham was said to have gotten numerous story ideas from conversations heard in ships' dining and smoking rooms. Evelyn Waugh's *Brideshead Revisited* and Katherine Ann Porter's *Ship of Fools* (set entirely aboard a German passenger ship on the eve of World War II) were among the many serious novels that made evocative use of the ocean liner setting.

Even the cramped confines of the stage found entertaining uses for luxury liner. Cole Porter put witty and exuberant words and music aboard a New

Left: In musical extravaganzas such as *Reaching for the Moon* (1931), set designers sought to impress audiences by exaggerating the already lush appointments of the great ships' interiors.

Below: Shipboard romance is one of the great modern fantasies. *Love Affair* (1939) dramatizes one such encounter where the lovers are played by Irene Dunne and Charles Boyer.

Opposite top: Hugh Grant peers through the porthole of his cabin in Roman Polanski's film, *Bitter Moon*. Rare now, in the past numerous films were set aboard luxury liners and cruise ships.

Opposite below: Before being broken up for scrap metal, the *Île de France* served as the setting for the movie *The Last Voyage* (1960), the fictional tale of the sinking of an ocean liner.

Left: Spencer Tracy (right), as the corrupt owner of a gambling ship, confronts a passenger on the grand staircase in the 1935 film *Dante's Inferno*. This morality tale climaxes with a shipboard fire which becomes a vision of hell for the protagonist and brings about his reform.

Above: The 1931 movie *Reaching for the Moon* was typical of the Hollywood productions that presented audiences with an ultra-glamorous depiction of a luxury liner passage, wherein life on board was an endless round of song, dance, romance, and cocktails.

Right: A ship's bar was a popular haven, especially for Americans frustrated by Prohibition. Romantic interludes were also possible, as portrayed here by Charles Boyer and Irene Dunne in *Love Affair*.

York-bound ship in the Broadway hit *Anything Goes*, and the considerably more downbeat play *Outward Bound* by Sutton Vane was a long-running success in the 1920s. Its setting of a gloomy ship turned out to be a metaphoric purgatory, with a passenger list of the dead.

But the movies were where the luxury liner lifestyle could be seen in its full opulence and glory. Fred Astaire and Ginger Rogers, dressed to the nines, spent most of the film *Shall We Dance* on an elegant Streamline Moderne liner, singing, dancing, and romancing to a selection of new tunes by George and Ira Gershwin.

Luxury ships were where romance was sparked for such stardusted couples as Clark Gable and Joan Crawford in *Chained*, Irene Dunne and Charles Boyer in *Love Affair*, Carole Lombard and Fred MacMurray in *The Princess Comes Across*, and Douglas Fairbanks and Bebe Daniels in the Art-Deco fantasia, *Reaching for the Moon*.

Hollywood's art directors tried to outdo the already extravagant real-life ships with sumptuously designed suites and nightclubs. Films such as *Reaching for the Moon* and *Transatlantic* presented their vessels as outlandish, opiated visions of hedonistic splendor. In the all-star *Big Broadcast of 1938*, two dazzling and imaginary super-streamlined ships raced to cross the Atlantic in two-and-a-half days, while the passengers enjoyed stage shows and flirted over cocktails at luxurious chrome-filled bars. In France, home to the most beautiful liners, they had no need for

Above: Hollywood depicted the shipboard romance, illicit or otherwise, in dozens of films such as *One Way Passage*, *History is Made at Night*, and *Love Affair*. Here, in Samuel Goldwyn's production of *Dodsworth*, a rich industrialist's wife (Ruth Chatterton) has an oceangoing fling with a European gigolo (David Niven).

Right: Now a classic film, the 1937 musical *Shall We Dance?* starred Fred Astaire and Ginger Rogers dancing to the music of George Gershwin aboard a stylishly streamlined white liner.

Opposite: The 1953 film *Titanic*. was the first of two major motion pictures released in the 1950s. The tragedy of the *Titanic* has through the years been the subject of numerous books, plays, songs, and poems—a new movie about the ship will be released in 1997.

Below: In a film like *Shall We Dance?* a ballet company on a sea voyage naturally leads to a major dance number on deck. Here, choreographer Hermes Pan instructs the corps de ballet while Edward Evertt Horton chats with a dancer.

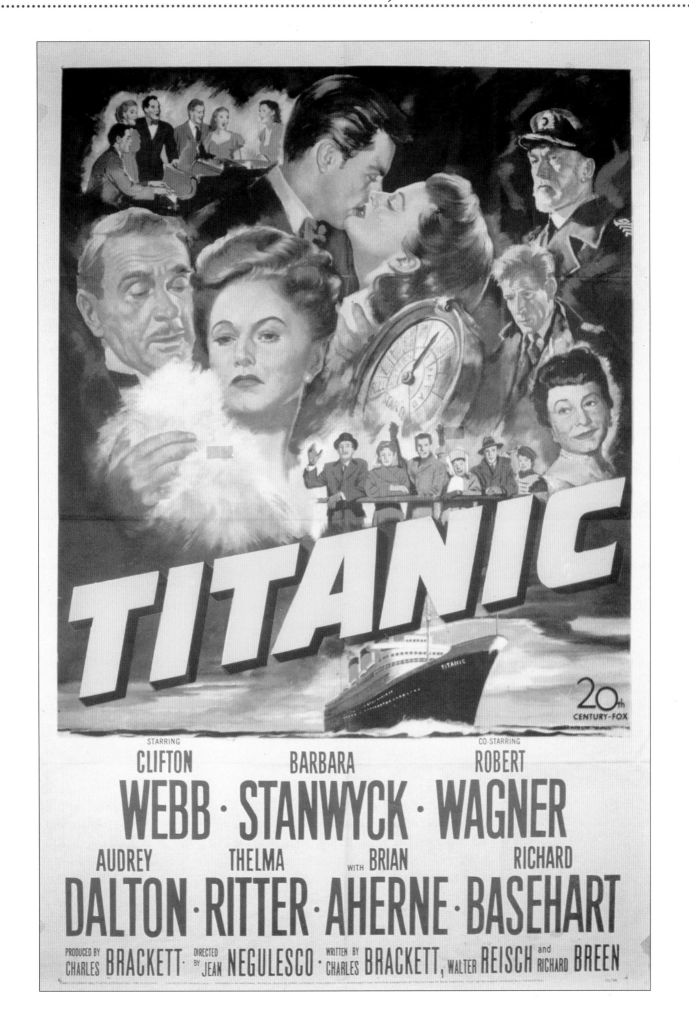

Right: One of the last of her
kind, the Cunard Line's *Queen
Elizabeth II* is shown here
departing from New York City,
where the World Trade Center
and the modern Manhattan skyline are visible in the background.

imaginary settings and used the actual *Normandie* for a Sacha Guitry
romantic comedy, *Les Perles de la Couronne*, with a climax in its
enormous—305-foot-long (94-meter)—dining room.

Although the shipping companies might not have liked it, Hollywood also
gave audiences vivid depictions of luxury liner disasters. Spectacular and
frightening sinkings were the memorable climaxes to such films as *Dante's
Inferno* and *History is Made at Night*. The sinking of the *Titanic* was
dramatized twice in the 1950s, once by Hollywood in the film called
Titanic and then by the British in *A Night to Remember*. The most
undeniably realistic depiction of a luxury liner's sinking was also the most
authentically poignant. The film was *The Last Voyage*, a fictional tale of
disaster striking a magnificent passenger ship. The magisterial *Ile de France*
herself, headed for the scrapheap after many decades of service, was
purchased by the film's producers in order to stage the action on her actual
decks and, in the end, to sink her before their cameras. It was a strange,
but fittingly unique end for both a legendary lady and the Golden Age of
ocean travel.

Left: Although primarily modern in design and decoration, the *Queen Elizabeth II*'s Yacht Club revives some of the style and mood of the shipboard cocktail bars of the "golden age."

$\mathcal{I}$NDEX